THE GREATEST MOMENTS OF THE WORLD CUP

by Kurt Waldendorf

CAPSTONE PRESS
a capstone imprint

Published by Capstone Press, an imprint of Capstone
1710 Roe Crest Drive, North Mankato, Minnesota 56003
capstonepub.com

Library of Congress Cataloging-in-Publication Data is available on the Library of Congress website

ISBN: 979-8-8752-6981-3 (hardcover)
ISBN: 979-8-8752-6976-9 (paperback)
ISBN: 979-8-8752-6977-6 (ebook PDF)

Summary: The World Cup is a thrilling spectacle of passes, shots, and scores. Readers explore some of the most memorable events to ever take place on a soccer pitch.

Editorial Credits
Editor: Heather DiLorenzo Williams, Designer, Cynthia Della-Rovere, Media Researchers, Courtney Rust, Catherine Guden

Image Credits
Getty: Allsport/Hulton Archive, 8, Ben Radford, 10–11, Buda Mendes, 14–15, Cameron Spencer, 4, Dave Cannon/Allsport/Hulton Archive, cover (middle), Duncan Raban/Allsport/Hulton Archive, 16, Jed Jacobsohn, 24, John Todd/ISI Photos/Getty Images, 25, Joern Pollex, 28–29, Jonathan Ferrey, cover (left), Julian Finney, 5, Kevin C. Cox, 12–13, Kevork Djansezian, cover (right), Keystone/Hulton Archive, 20–21, Lars Baron/Bongarts, cover (top), Paul Gilham, 7, Peter Robinson/EMPICS, 22, Popperfoto, 6, Richard Heathcote, 17, Robert Cianflone, 19, Newscom: Robert Vanden Brugge/UPI Photo Service, 26–27

Design Elements
Shutterstock: Arroyan Art, Dimitri Rukhlenko, Donglpix, madorf, Vector-3D

Printed and bound in China. 6459

CONTENTS

Chapter 1
WHAT MAKES A GREAT MOMENT ____ 4

Chapter 2
INDIVIDUAL MOMENTS __________ 6

Chapter 3
TEAM MOMENTS ______________ 18

Chapter 4
MOMENTS BEYOND
THE GAME ________________24

GLOSSARY 30
READ MORE 31
INTERNET SITES 31
INDEX 32
ABOUT THE AUTHOR 32

Words in **bold** are in the glossary.

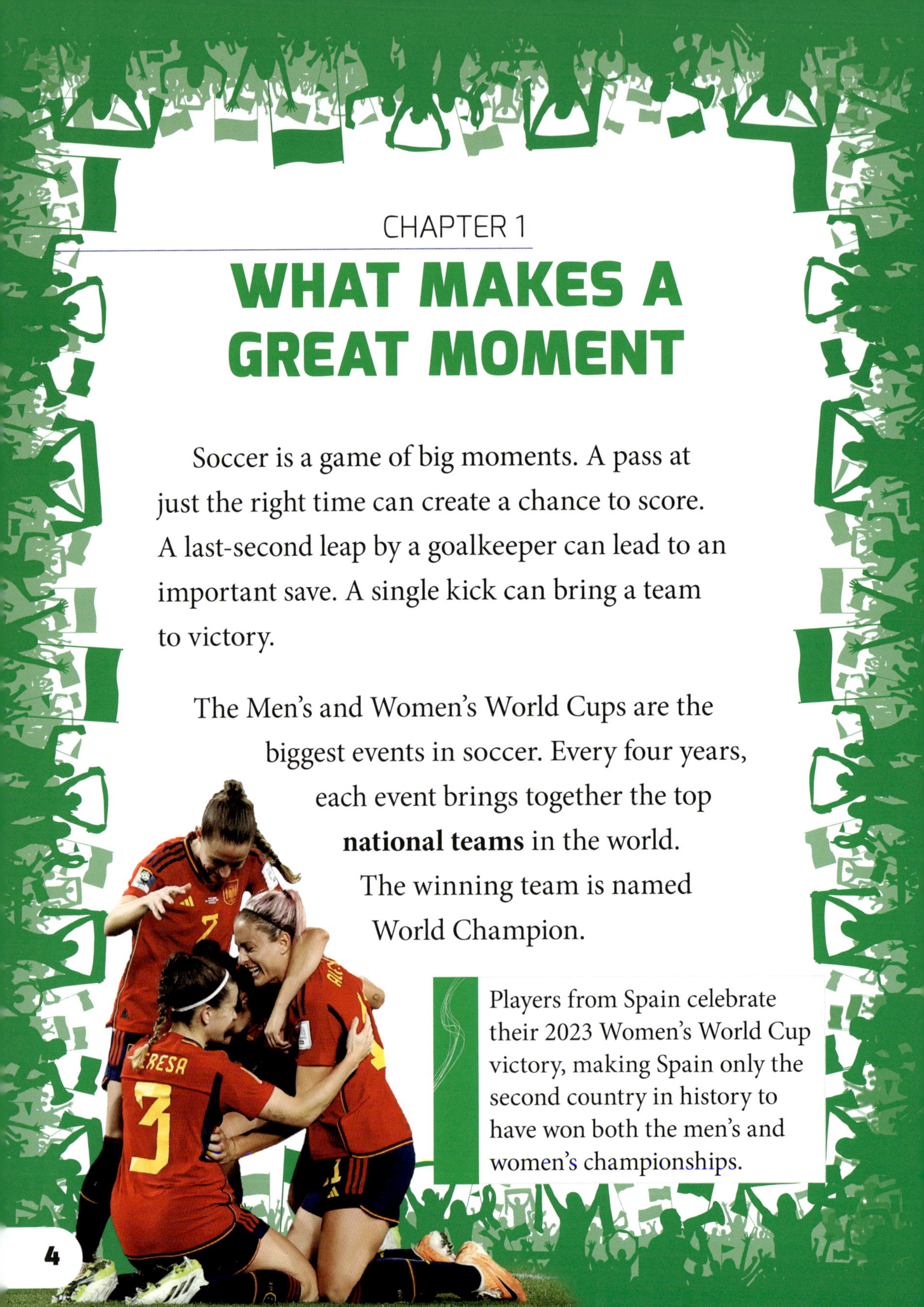

CHAPTER 1

WHAT MAKES A GREAT MOMENT

Soccer is a game of big moments. A pass at just the right time can create a chance to score. A last-second leap by a goalkeeper can lead to an important save. A single kick can bring a team to victory.

The Men's and Women's World Cups are the biggest events in soccer. Every four years, each event brings together the top **national teams** in the world. The winning team is named World Champion.

Players from Spain celebrate their 2023 Women's World Cup victory, making Spain only the second country in history to have won both the men's and women's championships.

Lionel Messi lifts the 2022 World Cup trophy after Argentina's defeat of France in the final.

Because the Men's and Women's World Cups are so special, many great moments happen at these events. These moments might involve players, teams, or even nations. But the greatest moments have one thing in common: fans remember them for many years to come.

CHAPTER 2

INDIVIDUAL MOMENTS

Some of the greatest World Cup moments are made by amazing individual performances.

Remarkable Youngsters

Brazilian soccer star Pelé created a great moment early in his career. He competed in his first Men's World Cup at age 17. Pelé dominated at the event. He scored a goal in the quarterfinals. In the semifinals, he scored a **hat trick**. But his best moment came in the final. Pelé's two goals led Brazil to victory. He became the youngest World Cup winner ever.

Pelé scores against Sweden during the 1958 World Cup final.

Marta takes a shot during the 2007 World Cup. She went on to become Brazil's top goal-scorer of all time.

Brazil's Marta had a similar performance in 2007. Coming into the Women's World Cup, the United States was a big favorite. But in the matchup between Brazil and the U.S. Women's National Team (USWNT), it was Marta who dominated. She scored two goals, and Brazil won 4–0. The match showed that 21-year-old Marta was already the top women's player in the world.

Diego Maradona played in four World Cup tournaments for Argentina. In 1986, he won the Golden Ball award as the tournament's best player.

Goal of the Century

Goals are often the most exciting moments of a match. One of the most memorable Men's World Cup goals happened in 1986. Argentina was playing its **rival**, England. Diego Maradona got the ball at midfield. He dribbled past English defenders. He sprinted toward the goal. Finally, he faked out the keeper and kicked the ball into the net.

The play took only 11 seconds. But Maradona passed five different defenders during his run. His incredible effort was later named the Goal of the Century.

A Tough Call

The 1986 Argentina-England matchup included a number of top moments. One came a few minutes into the second half. Diego Maradona leaped up to hit a ball with his head. England's keeper reached up to grab the ball with his hands. Somehow, the ball ended up in the back of the net. Video later showed that Maradona's hand had touched the ball. But the goal counted. The "Hand of God" goal is one of the most **controversial** in World Cup history.

An Ending Unlike Any Other

Some great plays are so unique that they never happen again. One of these plays came in the 2003 Women's World Cup final. In **extra time**, Germany's Nia Künzer scored a goal with her head. Normally, the match would continue after the goal. But the 2003 tournament was different. It had a "golden goal" rule: The first team to score in extra time won the match.

Künzer's goal was the only time a World Cup was decided by a golden goal. The rule changed in 2004. Teams now play the full extra time. If the score is tied, the match goes to **penalty kicks**.

Five World Cup finals have gone to penalty kicks. A penalty shootout decided the Women's World Cup in 1999 and 2011. The Men's World Cup was decided by penalty kicks in 1994, 2006, and 2022.

Nia Künzer (center) did not realize that her header had gone into the goal until she felt her teammates surround her seconds later.

Carli Lloyd's hat trick, including her midfield strike, occurred during the first 16 minutes of the 2015 final.

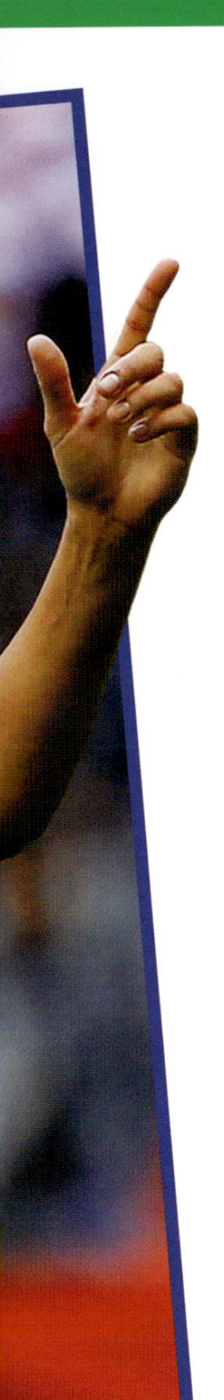

Jaw-Dropping Moves

Soccer is a game of style. Some great moments occur when players introduce moves few have seen before.

Johan Cruyff of the Netherlands created a new move in the 1974 Men's World Cup. Cruyff swung his leg to pass the ball. His defender leaped to the side. But the move was a fake out. Cruyff dribbled the ball the opposite way. The "Cruyff Turn" left the defender in the dust. The move was so useful that it is still taught today.

The USWNT's Carli Lloyd pulled off a shocking move in the 2015 Women's World Cup final. Lloyd got the ball at midfield. Everyone expected her to pass. Instead, she shot. Lloyd's strike flew 50 yards (46 m). It drifted over the keeper's fingers and into the net. The memorable goal capped an incredible three-goal day for Lloyd.

Argentina's Emi Martínez (right) blocks a shot from France's Randal Kolo Muani. Martínez earned the 2022 tournament's Golden Glove due to his amazing performance in the goal.

Game-Changing Saves

Not every memorable moment occurs on offense. Goalkeeper Emi Martínez stole the show with his defense in the 2022 Men's World Cup final. Argentina and France were tied with only seconds left in the match. A French player got past Argentina's defenders. He had a clear shot at the goal. But Martínez stretched out his foot at the last moment. His amazing save helped Argentina go on to win the tournament.

Kristine Lilly was not a goalkeeper. But she made one of the most memorable saves in Women's World Cup history. In the 1999 final, China came within inches of taking the lead against the United States. But Lilly leaped up from the goal line and knocked the shot away with her head. The play kept the USWNT in the match. The Americans went on to win the tournament.

Marco Tardelli celebrates his goal during the 1982 World Cup final.

Memorable Celebrations

Sometimes a player's reaction is the most memorable moment of a match. That was the case when Marco Tardelli scored for Italy at the 1982 Men's World Cup. Few people expected Italy to lead Germany 2–0 in the final. But no one looked more surprised than Tardelli. After scoring, he sprinted across the field. Tears ran down his cheeks. His joyful celebration became **iconic**.

Megan Rapinoe of the USWNT showed a different emotion during the 2019 Women's World Cup. Rapinoe was known for talking about off-the-field issues during her career. Some people criticized her for her words. But in her 2019 goal celebration, Rapinoe showed she did not care what people said about her. She stood tall with her arms wide. The pose showed she was proud to be herself.

Megan Rapinoe celebrates after scoring the first goal in the 2019 World Cup final.

CHAPTER 3

TEAM MOMENTS

Soccer is a team sport. Some of the greatest World Cup moments occur when teams achieve great things together.

A Shocking Upset

Jamaica was a big underdog at the 2023 Women's World Cup. The country had been to the tournament only once before. In 2023, Jamaica faced tough tests. The team needed to get past France and Brazil to advance.

The team was up to the challenge. Jamaica played to a tie with France after losing a player to a **red card**. They then also tied against Brazil. The 0–0 match was not the most exciting. But the result was shocking. It gave Brazil its earliest exit from the tournament since 1995. And it sent Jamaica to the second round for the first time.

Jamaica's Khadija Shaw (left) escapes a tackle by a French defender in the 2023 World Cup.

A Dominant Team

Some great moments come from players showing exceptional teamwork.

Brazil's 1970 men's team was full of star players. But the team's greatest moment was the result of working together. In the second half of the World Cup final against Italy, Brazil gracefully moved the ball up the field. They completed nine passes to eight different players. At the end of the play, Carlos Alberto knocked the ball into the net. The goal didn't just help Brazil win a World Cup title. It was one of the most impressive team goals in history.

FAST FACT

Brazil also had one of the biggest letdowns in Men's World Cup history. The team was the favorite in the 2014 tournament. But disaster struck in the semifinals against Germany. Brazil lost 7–1 in front of their home crowd.

Brazil's 1970 World Cup team is considered one of the greatest soccer teams of all time.

Johan Cruyff (left) and Franz Beckenbauer (right) were fierce rivals. Their very different styles helped shape soccer as it is played today.

A Heated Rivalry

Some great World Cup moments occur when rivals face off. One of the greatest men's rivalry moments took place between Germany and the Netherlands in 1974. Both teams were talented. And both had star players. Franz Beckenbauer led the German team. Johan Cruyff led the Netherlands squad. Each had dominated club leagues for years. In the World Cup final, they finally went head-to-head.

Fans for both countries filled the stands. The match lived up to the excitement. After going down 1–0, Germany battled back to win 2–1 and take home the title.

FAST FACT

Rivalries between neighboring countries are known as "border battles." Germany and the Netherlands and Argentina and Brazil are heated border battles in the men's game. The United States and Canada have a strong rivalry in women's soccer.

CHAPTER 4

MOMENTS BEYOND THE GAME

Some World Cup moments are memorable for their importance off the field.

Playing for the Home Crowd

The 1999 Women's World Cup was a big event for women's soccer. The sport had grown since the first Women's World Cup in 1991. But for the 1999 tournament, organizers made huge plans. They set up matches in large stadiums across the United States. It was a big risk. Would enough people show up to fill the stadiums?

Mia Hamm's amazing skills drew many new fans to soccer after the 1999 World Cup.

The 90,185 fans at the 1999 Women's World Cup final set a record at the time for the biggest crowd ever to gather for a women's sporting event.

Fans responded. Nearly 80,000 people showed up to the USWNT's first match. The crowd was the biggest ever for a women's sporting event in the United States. Fans broke the record again at the World Cup final. More than 90,000 cheered as the USWNT took on China. The moment showed that given the chance, fans would show up to support women's soccer.

A Tense Match

Players at the World Cup don't just represent their teams. They also represent their countries. Because of this, some moments are **political**.

The United States faced Iran at the 1998 Men's World Cup. The relationship between the two

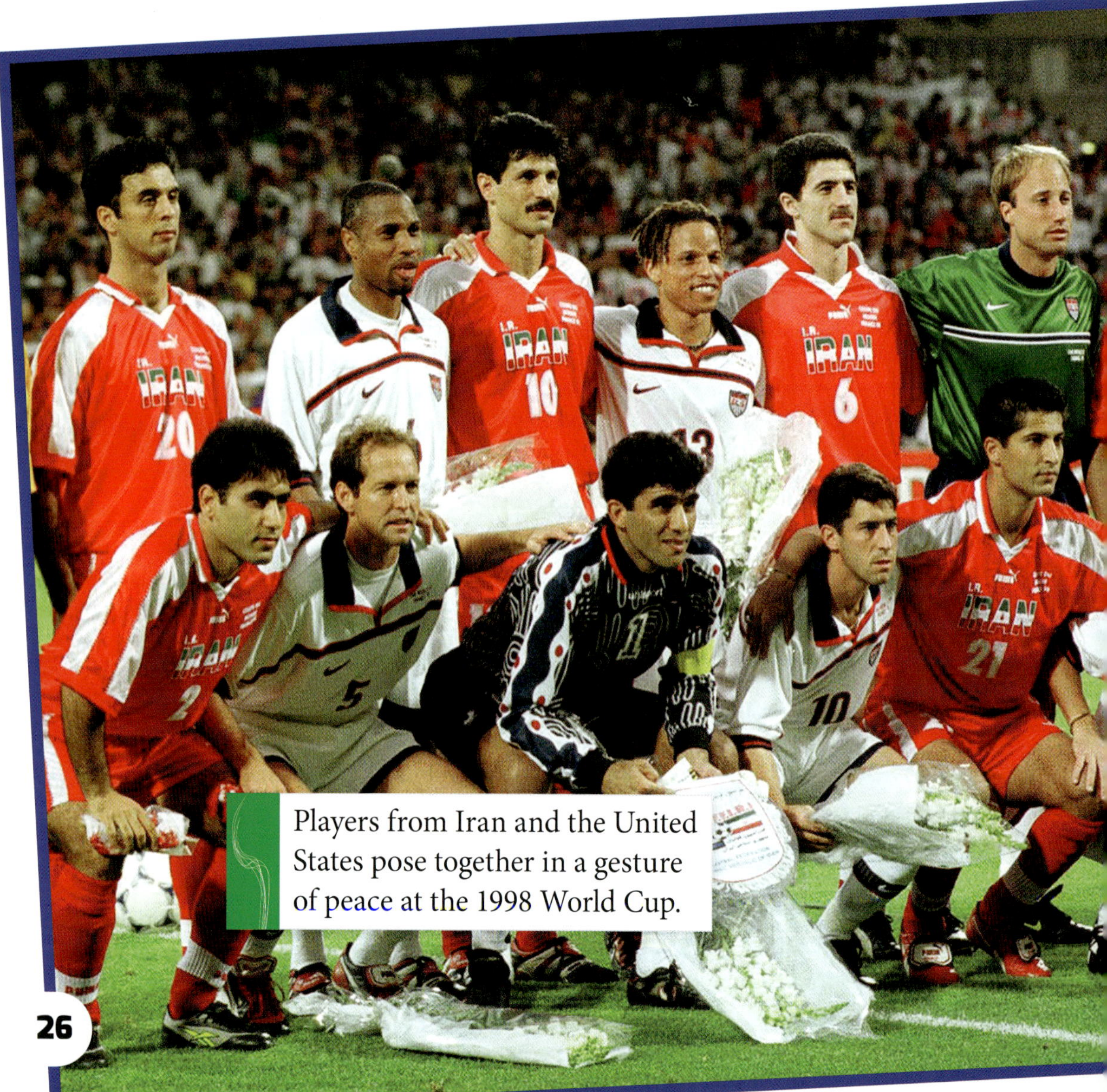

Players from Iran and the United States pose together in a gesture of peace at the 1998 World Cup.

countries was bad at the time. But the teams showed great **sportsmanship**. Iran's players gave U.S. players white roses before the match. The flowers stood for peace. The players took photos together. The moment showed the power of sports to bring people together.

A Tough Call

The team from England became known for sportsmanship at the 2023 Women's World Cup. English players did not boast after winning. They showed respect and support for opponents. The team's ability to win with grace became one of the biggest storylines of the tournament.

A Much-Needed Win

When a team wins at the World Cup, fans from all over the team's home country celebrate.

In 2011, people in Japan needed something to celebrate. An earthquake and tsunami had just hit the nation. Many cities had been destroyed. Japan's women's national team delivered hope. The underdogs made it all the way to the Women's World Cup final.

Players from Japan's women's national team celebrate their 2011 World Cup victory. They were the first team from Asia to win either the men's or women's tournament.

Then they did something extraordinary. Japan beat the heavily favored U.S. women's team to bring the nation its first World Cup title. The win wasn't only a huge upset. It was also a much-needed moment of happiness for the people of Japan.

Future Moments

What great moments will take place at the next World Cup? It's impossible to predict. But one thing is for sure. Fans will remember them for many years afterward.

GLOSSARY

controversial (kon-truh-VUR-shuhl)—causing a lot of argument

extra time (EK-stra TYM)—an additional period of play when a match is tied after regular time

hat trick (HAT TRIK)—when a player scores three goals in one game

iconic (eye-CAHN-ik)—widely viewed as perfectly capturing the meaning or spirit of something or someone

national teams (NASH-uh-nuhl TEEMZ)—sports squads that represent their countries

penalty kicks (PEN-uhl-tee KICKZ)—free kicks awarded to the offense when the defense commits a penalty

political (puh-LIT-uh-kuhl)—of or relating to the government

red card (RED KARD)—a penalty that ejects a player from a match

rival (RYE-vuhl)—someone who a person competes against

sportsmanship (SPORTS-muhn-ship)—fair and respectful behavior when playing a sport

READ MORE

Flynn, Brendan. *The World Soccer Encyclopedia.* Minneapolis. ABDO, 2025.

Shaw, Gina. *What Is the Women's World Cup?* New York. Penguin, 2023.

Streeter, Anthony. *World Cup All-Time Greats.* Mendota Heights, MN. North Star Editions, 2024.

INTERNET SITES

Britannica Kids: Women's World Cup
kids.britannica.com/kids/article/Womens-World-Cup/638782

Britannica Kids: World Cup
kids.britannica.com/kids/article/World-Cup/390872

ESPN: World Cup
www.espn.com/soccer/league/_/name/fifa.world

TIME for Kids: World Cup
www.timeforkids.com/g34/?text=World+Cup

U.S. Soccer
www.ussoccer.com/

INDEX

Argentina, 5, 9, 14, 23

Beckenbauer, Franz, 23
Brazil, 6–7, 18, 20, 23

Canada, 23
China, 15, 25
Cruyff, Johan, 13, 23

England, 9, 27

France, 14, 18

Germany, 10, 17, 20, 23

Iran, 26–27
Italy, 17, 20

Jamaica, 18
Japan, 28–29

Künzer, Nia, 10

Lilly, Kristine, 15
Lloyd, Carli, 12–13

Maradona, Diego, 9
Marta, 7
Martínez, Emi, 14

Netherlands, 13, 23

Pelé, 6

Rapinoe, Megan, 17

Tardelli, Marco, 17

United States, 7, 15, 23–24, 26
U.S. Women's National Team (USWNT), 7, 13, 15, 17, 25

About the Author

Kurt Waldendorf is the author of more than a dozen books for children. When he's not writing or editing, he enjoys indoor rock climbing and running along the shore of Lake Michigan with his dog. He lives in Chicago.